BLACK SHEEP SECRET
The Homosexual Spirit Exposed

James Bligen

authorHOUSE®

AuthorHouse™
1663 Liberty Drive, Suite 200
Bloomington, IN 47403
www.authorhouse.com
Phone: 1-800-839-8640

First published by AuthorHouse 5/9/2008

ISBN: 978-1-4343-5160-9 (sc)

Library of Congress Control Number: 2008902816

Printed in the United States of America
Bloomington, Indiana

This book is printed on acid-free paper.

All scripture reference is from the King James version of the Bible.

To Mildred Elaine Riley:

Thank you for standing in prayer with me through all my life struggles. For encouraging me in my weakest moments, and telling me the truth. Thanks for being wise enough to speak to my need.

CONTENTS

Introduction

STRAIGHT TALK

And what he hath seen and heard, that he testifieth;
and no man receiveth his testimony.

St. John 3:32

The common mistake most, so-called heterosexual men make when they are engaged in homosexual sex, is that by doing this they are not gay, or will not become gay. However, it is the nature of this spirit to infiltrate one's life, and break down the lines of compromise.

We are so into protecting ourselves that we are willing to dress up our bad habits to make them look good. Now a man that sleeps with other men is Gay period. Whether or not he is on the "Down Low" does not matter. If he sleeps with men, there is a homosexual spirit involved. Men on the Down Low are simply closet homosexuals.

Men who sleep with woman and men, who are not married are called bisexuals. Somehow this has become more acceptable. You see it on talk shows all the time. Men and women come on these shows and say: "I'm bisexual." The audience claps their hands in approval and perhaps you were one of these audience members. Even if you were watching at home, you were willing to accept this fact.

Once homosexuality becomes acceptable to you, it is more likely that you will engage in the act.

The tragedy is that I have heard with my own ears women say:

"He is not gay. He just likes having sex with men."

Wakeup, Spirits are transferable and homosexuality is a spirit whether you believe it or not.

It all starts with compromise. It is impossible to know what any one person will do if the right situation presents it's self. Desperate people do desperate things.

This is very dangerous in the congregation, because we are so repressed about sex. We give antidotal messages about sex and as it were cover it with a bandage, but never delve deep into the heart, or the spirit of it. Now a single man not willing to risk getting a woman pregnant will want to have sex in her rectum, or turn to a homosexual to get a release, and unbeknownst to him gets a snare to his heart. He doesn't know or understand that he has opened the door to demon spirits. Nor do men understand that when they desire to see two women engage in sex, they are actually entertaining the spirit of homosexuality.

This is not a spirit you can say a few tongues over and expect to be delivered. This is not a spirit that you can say a few prayers for, and expect to be made free.

This is a strong hold, and in order to be made free you must first get tired of it.

Your mind needs to be changed. You need to be changed in the spirit of your mind, and then deliverance will come.

How can I tell if my man is sleeping with another man? What are the signs to look for?

Many women want to understand homosexuality, and they should. However, homosexuality is a spirit, and homosexuality is the last thing on women's mind when they start to date a man, however it should be the first. There are seven signs that identify a man engaging in sex with a man.

It is not important to know the why, or how two men can engage in sex together. However, to answer this age-old question you must first understand the spirit of possession. Homosexuality is in its simplest form possession. However, if you will not acknowledge the fact that it is a spirit. How can you understand the why? It is written:

> *If I have told you earthly things, and ye believe not, how*
> *shall ye believe, if I tell you of heavenly things?*
> *St. John 3:12*

Homosexuality and men on the "Down Low" has grown at alarming rates. Therefore, women who are just interested in getting married; don't take enough time to get to know the man they are with. In addition, they don't know if they are gay or on the "Down Low". Then when they find out, they are devastated, and begin to feel less than a woman, because they didn't take the time to investigate the man they married.

Still some who were recently saved, are so eager to get married so they won't have an urge, and not have someone there to scratch it for them. Therefore, they are willing to marry the first man willing to say: "I do". They've known the guy for three weeks, and now they want to get married, and just because he has had sex with her she is convinced he is not gay, or on the "Down Low". Now because he looks straight, acts straight, and says he can't stand fagots they believe he's not gay. Wake up! Don't you think he protests too much?

It is time that women get their heads out of the clouds about this issue. It is time that men stop making excuses for their desire to sleep with men, and Black Sheep Secret is the book to help them do it.

Chapter 1

THE TESTIMONY

"And they overcame him by the blood of the Lamb, and by the word of their testimony; and they loved not their lives unto the death."

Revelation 12:11

In 1995, 1.3 million children were sexually assaulted in the United States (Child Lures Prevention Web site). The Child Lures Prevention Web site also states that 89 percent of child sexual assault cases involve persons known to the child, such as a caretaker or family acquaintance. Many of these children go on to become homosexuals and lesbians with issues of guilt, depression, anger, hatred, self-loathing, and a lack of self-confidence.

My own experience with molestation and homosexuality began with a close family member. I was four or five years old, and we slept in the same room, in the same bed, queen size as I remember.

I didn't know what I was doing, only that I was obeying this person's commands. We did this until someone knocked on the door and started to open it. He then threw me off him and wrapped the covers over us and acted as if nothing happened.

I Love Lucy was playing on the black-and-white console television as I wondered about what had just transpired. This would be the last time this person would touch me in this manner. Perhaps he felt bad about it; however, the damage was done. I was four or five years old.

Please understand that the tip of a young boy's penis is just as sensitive as a man's. That is why you see some small boys playing between their legs when they turn three and four years of age. Even at this tender age, the penis can be made to become erect.

Anyway, as I thought about the events that had recently transpired, I considered that the feeling was good, and I was willing to do it again, because now he had taught me that this was right.

A young lady used to babysit me. She was a teenager about seventeen years old. She laid me on top of her, causing my hips to move back and forth while her hips moved under me. However, since I had already learned this lesson from another family member, it had become child's play. Children gravitate to the evil long before they are taught or guided to the good.

In both cases, there were no penetration, but the stench and stigma of molestation had placed its mark on me.

While there are worse stories of molestation,

> anytime anyone exposes himself or herself to a child in a
> sexual manner that is molestation.

This would manifest itself again a few days or weeks later when my mother and I were in bed together (we were living with one of her friends and therefore shared a room). I took her hand and repeated what I had been taught: My mother woke up, moved her hand, and looked at me, but never said a word, and I never told her what had been happening to me (in the case of my babysitter) for quite some time.

In the next couple of years, my mother and I would move to Hilton Head Island, South Carolina. I would have more encounters with men, as I would soon come to find out.

My mother and I lived with my grandmother at the time, and I was the only boy in the house. Four young ladies were also living there, and we grew up like sisters and brother. My mother was not one to let me hang out with the boys in the neighborhood. She often made me stay home, which meant that I would have to play with the girls unless the boys came to our house. There were many days when I played with paper dolls.

I remember when my mother went to a family member's home and took me along with her. While she was talking inside, I was playing outside. I was about seven years old. Then a much older gentleman came over and saw me outside. As I look back on it now he had to be about twenty-five years old or more.

He sat down on the ground where no one could see us, pulled out his penis, and told me to place my mouth on it. When I refused, he said he would give me five dollars if I would do it for him. I then placed my mouth on his penis, and he tried to push it further into my mouth. As I began to choke, he took his penis out of my mouth long enough for me to catch my breath and then told me to do it again.

This would go on for a few years. Each time this person saw me he would tell me to do the same thing. I remember when I was in the fourth grade he held me up from class just so I would perform oral sex on him. He would always bring something I wanted to bribe me into rendering him this service. Over time, this would prove to have a lasting effect on me and would begin my life of secrets, lies, and destruction.

I tried to live a normal life in spite of what had already transpired. As I started school, I had a new battlefield to cross: teasing, belittling, and anger.

> School is where I first heard the words "homosexual" and "faggot."

Even before I knew what the words meant, children were telling me this is who I was.

Adults were no better. In the place where I should find comfort and love is where I found the most hatred, misunderstanding, and cruelty. By the time I was in the third grade, I had attempted suicide inside my classroom by cutting myself at my wrist but missed the main artery, or so I was told. I was sent to the office of the school nurse, who cleaned the wound and bandaged me up. I don't remember my mother addressing it with me at home or even mentioning it to me ever. I now know that I was crying out for help, but I never received the help I needed.

Back then teachers didn't call child welfare for every cause. The parent was more important then, and teachers would call the parent to deal with a problem with their child. Today, if you sneeze too hard at a child, child welfare could be called.

Frequently a family member would come to visit my grandmother. On one visit she said to me, "It's a shame that we have a faggot in the family."

While this did hurt me, it was minimal compared to what I had already been through, and somehow I gained the strength to go on.

Through the years, my mother and I would drift farther and farther apart, which would leave me vulnerable. By the time, I was ten, I had a stiff upper lip. No one was going to walk over me because they didn't like what they thought I was. Therefore, I began to fight back.

I remember when another family member in particular would visit. In my mind, she came down just to make my life miserable. It seemed that every time she came down we would get into an argument. One time we even fought fist to fist because I thought my life was in the balance. Not that she wanted to kill me, but I felt I had to stand up for myself, because no one else had or would. I even fought with my teachers, and by this time, my grades were slipping.

Back then my family was not big on telling each other how they felt about one another. I don't remember one time hearing my mother say, "I love you," when I was growing up. My aunts didn't say it, my uncles were never around to say it, and I had no way of identifying it.

As the years went by, I began to hate my father for what he did to me.

I would often think about that day and connect it to why I was attracted to boys, and I hated him.

I was teased because I wasn't very masculine. Being raised in a family of woman with no outlet to express myself as a young man was difficult. There were no male figures around, at least not on a regular basis, and this added to my frustration. How could I learn what being a man meant without having a man around to teach me?

What I saw of men in the neighborhood was that they were womanizers, drunkards, and drug users; men who were looking for what was between a woman's legs and not what's in her heart; men who thought getting a woman pregnant made them a man but didn't think that raising a baby was a man's job. And I knew I didn't want to be like that, and I hated men for it.

OK, so how can I hate a gender that I am a member of? Nothing I had ever seen of men endeared me to the species.

I had dreams of being with a woman. I mean, I still liked women and wanted to be with a girl. However, if I didn't love myself, how was I going to show love to someone else? However, Jesus was letting me know that he loved me.

In the South, all the members of a family went to the same church, and if you were in that family you were expected to be a part of that church also. When I became ten years old, I told my mother that I wanted to join the church. Back then Baptist churches in my hometown had services on certain Sundays, and our church was closed on this particular Sunday. My mother called a cousin of ours and asked that she take me to her church because I wanted to join our family church.

See, back then, if your regular church service was not scheduled for a particular Sunday, you could go to another service, and when the altar call was made you would go to the altar and give your hand to the preacher. He would then ask you what church you wanted to join. Of course, I named my family's church.

However, as I stepped before the altar I felt an arm wrap around my shoulders from the right side and a hand on my left shoulder. As this hand rested on my left shoulder I felt a touch that melted my heart.

> I turned swiftly and looked to my left, thinking I would see
> a hand on my shoulder, and saw nothing.

I turned to my right, and still there was no one, yet someone had touched me. As I turned to face the preacher, again I felt tears filling my eyes. I immediately drew back the tears fearing that the congregation would think I was silly, but I left that service knowing that Jesus had touched me. The feeling I took from that experience was what I can only describe now as pure love, and it was the first time in my life that I felt loved.

I went on with my life, becoming increasingly angry with my mother for not protecting me. I spent most of my time stealing, lying, cheating, and being very disobedient. I ran away twice, was kicked out of my mother's home more times than I can count, and had more in common with animals than people. And yet God would always have someone to show me what love and family was all about.

Finally, I met a young lady who showed me all the love a young man could want, or so I thought. As I grew to know her family, I found that her mother was a pastor of a sanctified church. As time went on, I fell in love with this young lady and began to attend church with her and her mother. One night when we went to Savannah, Georgia, to a church service where I learned firsthand about praising the Lord.

As service got started, they began to sing songs and clap their hands. Seeing this I started clapping my hands. After all, the singing did sound good. After a while I heard the pastor yell out my name and cry, "Praise the Lord!"

Well, I didn't know what she was talking about, but she continued, "Say thank you, Jesus! Hallelujah."

I stood there looking to see whom she was talking to but soon found out that she was talking to me. Of course, you know that by this time I couldn't wait until the end of service.

Finally the end of service came. I don't remember the message, but I do remember what my girlfriend's mother said to me as I left the church.

She said, "Do you know what that was?"

I replied, "What!"

She said, "That was the Holy Ghost."

I replied, "I didn't want that!"

She answered, "Well he wants you."

I walked away in disbelief. However, God was not finished with me yet. The next day I remember being drawn to this Jesus. I knew his name but not what he was about, and I had to find out who this Jesus was. I read anything I could find with Jesus on it. I mean

> I read comic strips and I read the New Testament and whatever else I could get my hands on that would shed some light on this Jesus.

I just felt this thing inside me driving me to learn about his life. What I felt could only be described as pure love. The exact feeling I had felt only six years earlier standing before a Baptist preacher was here again, and this time it was here to stay. I was sixteen years old.

At this time, I was living on the streets, sleeping in abandoned cars and homes. I was not able to take a shower or change clothes on a regular basis, and this was in the dead of winter. In the morning, my girlfriend would let me wash up at her mom's home and would fix me something to eat. I did this for a few days, until one night I gave my heart to God. This was on a Friday night. The next day a large truck pulled up with a load of boxes filled with clothes, and I was able to fill up a bag with clothes that fit me perfectly. God is so good.

Later that day my girlfriend's sister told me I could come stay with her and her family. They had an extra room and welcomed me to stay with them. As you could imagine, I was so thankful. I went to her house and she showed me a large room beautifully adorned with a full-size bed. That night I went to bed, and it felt as if I was sleeping on clouds. A week later, I received the gift of the Holy Ghost in this same room.

So this should be the end of my turmoil, right? No!

> I was saved, filled with the Holy Ghost, and still dealt with
> feelings of homosexuality.

I was still attracted to boys as well as girls, still addicted to sex, still looking for love.

In December of the same year, the Lord led me to New York City.

By this time, I had learned to hate my mother, because she was never around to protect me. To get attention I would steal and tell lies only because I knew it would force her to pay attention to me, even if it was the wrong attention. I had watched her laugh and play with other people's children; yet she rarely had a gentle word to say to me.

Therefore, I found myself in New York City, saved and filled with the Holy Ghost. Seventeen years old and still angry, still hurting, with feelings of rejection and craving for love; the love I felt was never present with my mother. I knew that Jesus loved me, but at the time, I couldn't completely accept it, because I didn't love myself.

I was thanking God for being safe from my past and past experiences and soon found out that I was not safe.

In the church is where I found that homosexuality is alive
and well.

It was through church that I encountered my first willing gay sexual experience—with someone who had been saved and filled with the Holy Ghost longer than me. He came to visit me, and with my naïve, country, gullible self, I didn't see what his true intentions were until he planted a solid kiss on my lips, driving his tongue into my mouth and putting his hands into my pants and stroking my penis.

It was easy to let go and allow him to pull off my clothes and do all that he was doing to me, because for the first time someone was including me. They weren't taking away my control. I had a choice, and for the first time I chose to allow it, I chose to like it, and I chose eventually to pursue it.

Eventually I would fall in love (lust) with a guy around my age, which would take me years to overcome. However, God had a plan for my life.

By 1985 I had fallen into many hurtful lusts, because I began to believe the voice of the enemy, which said: "You will never make it to the end." From there,

I spent many years in and out of the Lord trying to please
people instead of pleasing God.

However, in all of that, God had a plan for my life, and it led me to repentance.

In 1993, I was living in Jersey City, New Jersey. One Sunday morning I woke up and decided to go back to church after months of feeling tired of the gay bar scene and no longer feeling fulfilled in the very thing that once brought me so much happiness; or so I thought.

I got up, took a shower, and proceeded to get dressed for service, when all of a sudden I started crying and couldn't stop. I cried all the way to the church and through service. I was in the process of being made free. I dedicated my life back to God in my heart on that day. It was the first time I made up my mind to serve the Lord without reservation.

Many of us serve God with partiality: Lord, you can have this, but I'll keep this to myself; or I will do this, but I won't do that.

Nothing was going to stop me. I threw away all the phone numbers I had for gay men. I gave up all my gay friends and anything that would remind me of that lifestyle. I was ready to serve the Lord with everything within me, because

> unless you are willing to give up the past, you can never
> be free from it,

and I wanted to be free.

It took me ten years after I was saved and filled with the Holy Ghost to receive deliverance, ten years of backsliding, ten years before I got tired of the way I was living. I was tired of lies, I told myself, tired of being told lies by my suitors, tired of being with a different person every night, and tired of trying to make a relationship work with someone I was never supposed to be with in the first place. I wanted to be free.

Ten years, one marriage, one divorce, two children, and all hope lost. Still saved, still filled, yet preaching, yet praying, and trying to keep this deep dark secret.

Then in January the following year at a service in the Bronx, the Lord spoke these words to me:

> *"Your earthly father placed it on you (homosexuality), but*
> *your Heavenly Father is taking it off of you."*

It was at this moment when I knew I was delivered, free, and whole from homosexuality. Thank you, Jesus!

Why would the Lord say to me, "Your earthly father placed it on you"?

Because this is how I felt. If he didn't touch me, perhaps I wouldn't have been receptive to other touches from men. More than that, if I felt empowered as a child perhaps I would've been able to say no and tell my mother what had taken place. As it is, my mother went to her grave never knowing the pain I had suffered and the agony I endured. However, God blessed me many years before her death to reconnect with my mother. It was a relationship I always dreamed of having with her. We had many good times together, and even though I was not with her in person when she died, I was with her in spirit.

Chapter 2

THE SPIRIT OF HOMOSEXUALITY

"Wisdom is the principal thing; therefore get wisdom:
and with all thy getting get <u>understanding</u>."

Proverbs 4:7

It is very easy for us to look on a man who is effeminate and judge him as a homosexual instead of searching out the matter and finding out what has transpired in this man's life to make him abandon his masculinity. In other words, let's get to the heart of the matter and search the spirit of it.

Homosexuality is a spirit. No one is born with it, and "once a homosexual" does not mean that you will always be one, at least not in God, for He has made a way of escape.

Perhaps you have heard a homosexual say, "I was born a homosexual." This is not an accurate statement.

Through my own deliverance and intimacy with the Lord, I have come to understand that at the moment of birth (directly after birth), there are demon assassins assigned to each of us. We now can understand that it is not at conception or in the womb that the enemy attacks, but at birth. This is the reason why some gay persons can say, "I always knew there was something different about me." The Bible has said:

"...I will not again curse the ground any more for man's sake; for
the imagination of man's heart is evil from his youth..."

Genesis 8:21

The Bible says that from youth the imagination of man's heart is evil, not from the womb or conception.

What this means is that not only are we conceived in sin and shaped in iniquity, but we also have demon spirits that the devil assigns to us. Therefore, whatever you personally have had to deal with from a child is the effect of demon assassins that the devil has prepared to destroy your destiny. Then situations align themselves so that these spirits can work in your life. This is the birth of generational curses.

Now a demon spirit of homosexuality, prostitution, or murder marks himself with a baby. Then as this baby grows, this spirit causes situations to arise in his or her life to lead them into a lifestyle that will feed that particular spirit.

If we believe the scripture that says:

> *"Before I formed you in the belly I knew you."*
>
> *Jeremiah 1:5*

Then we could surmise that God knew each one of us before the foundation of the world; this is the reason Jesus came onto the Earth, because he knew us from the foundation of the world and loved us. If then God knew us from the foundation of the Earth, it is only wise to assume that Satan knew of us also. More simplistic, we could surmise that Satan is angry with man, because the scripture says:

> *"Therefore rejoice you heavens, and you that dwell in them. Woe to the inhabitants of the earth and of the sea! For the devil is come down to you, having great wrath, because he knows that he has but a short time."*
>
> *Revelation 12:1*

Why is he angry with man? Simply put, man was made in the image of God. It is also the reason why gay males are less accepted by the public than gay women.

OK, so Satan is angry with God and therefore is angry with man because man looks like God, and God has already said:

"You shall not lie with man kind as with woman kind: it is abomination."
Leviticus 18:22

Knowing that homosexuality is an abomination to God, Satan now has the avenue he needs to destroy the image of God. You would say to me, "How does Satan know what is an abomination to God?"

Satan is the opposite of God, everything that is a lie is of the devil. For the scripture has said:

"...He was a murderer from the beginning, and abode not in the truth, because there is no truth in him. When he speaks a lie, he speaks of his own: for he is a liar, and the father of it."
St. John 8:44

Do you not know that while God was giving Moses the commandments, Satan was there seeking an opportunity to destroy them? For Satan is the accuser of the brethren. However, homosexuality was on the Earth long before God gave Moses the commandments. It is part of the reason that God destroyed Sodom and Gomorra. Homosexuality is a lie and therefore is of the devil.

Why is it that women lying with woman in the Bible is only confusion, but men lying with men is abomination?

When two men come together and pass their seed from one to another, they become a part of each other. This act is abomination. This is why you have men when they are having sex with woman wanting to sodomize their wives, because that spirit is still in them. Then when they see the guys they have been with, something moves inside of them, because the spirit of that man is still in them. The man has allowed another man to become a part of him. It is also why men who have been sodomized will continually begin to exhibit feminine gestures, because in the grand design man was designed for women.

When a man then leaves the woman and begins to sodomize a man, that man (who is being sodomized) will begin to exhibit feminine mannerisms, because he has allowed himself to become a receptor instead of a projector.

Women do not have an apparatus that will transfer seed from their body to another woman, nor do they possess seed. They have eggs and therefore could never be a part of one another. This is why the act of woman being with woman sexually is confusion.

In other words, the woman's body is designed to receive of the man. It is the seed of a man that is responsible for the fertilization of a woman's egg and is spiritually the beginning of life. For God has placed life in the seed; however, the seed is not complete by itself. This means that even the egg of a woman is designed to receive of the man, whereas the man's body is designed to penetrate the woman's body, and his seed is designed to penetrate her egg.

The Bible never addresses women's eggs as seed; however, the man's sperm is always addressed as seed, or seed of copulation, because of the planting into woman. In this regard, the woman is in the place of Earth from which the man was taken.

> God gave the woman as a helpmeet to man, and woman was taken out of man, becoming a natural part of him; thus creating the family.

When a man leaves the woman and turns to a man, he rejects himself as the head to God, being made in the image of God, and makes himself as the weaker vessel in the image of woman. It is as if you say man was taken from man or woman from woman. The two cancel out each other. For God has said:

> *"Be fruitful and multiply, and replenish the earth, and subdue it:*
> *and have dominion over the fish of the sea, and over the fowl of the*
> *air, and over every living thing that moves upon the earth.*
>
> *Genesis 1:28*

Two men can't multiply nor can two women multiply, and two men coming together make a mockery of God.

Please understand that God does not hate the man who is a homosexual. He hates what homosexuals do. The act of sodomy and the sexual intimacy between two men or two women is what God hates.

Homosexuality is derived from the spirit of lust. If one were to look into the lifestyle of the gay male, they would find that sex takes up approximately 70 percent or more of their life. If they are not having it, they are thinking about it. It is the underlying driving force behind most of their relationships. Lust is often confused with love in the gay male's life. This is true of the homosexual male and heterosexual male alike. It is also the reason why homosexuality seems so hard to overcome, because men find it hard to overcome their own feelings of lust. This is why you find grown men still touching themselves, and if you don't do the same, they say you must be gay. It is also why some men have sex with multiple partners even when they are married.

> The enemy takes the natural drive of a man to procreate
> and perverts it.

Add in a few suggestive actions like molestation or time in prison, and even the most hardened heterosexual may be tempted into having some kind of relationship with another man. This is why you have married men living on the down low.

The devil has made it so easy; all one would have to say to a male living under the influence of lust is, "Do you want to have sex?" The answer is usually yes, homosexual or not.

What one must understand about men living under the influence of lust for the most part is that he is about getting to it. He can learn how to prolong the foreplay to make you feel good, but the underlining point for him in most cases is to get right to it. Therefore, he wines and dines you. He says the most wonderful things, all in the attempt to get to the goods, and those persons who have never heard anyone tell them anything of value fall prey to these cunning words.

I myself have fallen prey to many wise devised fables designed only to get you where they want you, and when all is said and done, you are left holding the emotional baggage.

The only thing that separates a heterosexual male from a homosexual male is who they lie with; but the extent each will go to in order to lie with their perspective partner is the same.

Homosexuality is so rampant because men don't play games with each other. They don't have to wine and dine each other to get to sex. They are sexually driven and therefore can bypass all of the pleasantries and get right into sex. However, there are exceptions to this rule. Homosexuals who take on the persona of a woman will want to be wined and dined. They will need to be caressed and hear those wise devised fables that some men speak so well. In addition, in recent years some women have taken an active role in the way they express themselves sexually. It seems as if the women are becoming more aggressive about sex while the man is becoming more subdued.

We will not stop this spirit with hurtful words and demeaning stares. My godmother helped me by loving me. She told me the truth, but she never treated me any differently, and when she spoke the word, she pulled no punches. She allowed the seed of the word to penetrate my spirit and change my mind. No doubt she went down on her knees on my behalf, and she never turned her back on me. She sought me where I was and always greeted me with a hug.

She challenged my world views and brought out the best things in me. Then when the Lord delivered me, she rejoiced with me.

I honor you, Mildred Elaine Riley, for being a true mother of Zion and a Proverbs 31 woman.

Chapter 3

Homosexuals in the Church

"I beseech you therefore, brethren, by the mercies of God, that ye present your bodies a living sacrifice, holy acceptable unto God, which is your reasonable service."

Romans 12:1

The notion that homosexuals are in the church is not new. Years ago you could spot a gay male a mile away. Today you can't tell who is who or what is what. Gay males have become such experts at hiding their sexual orientation that you need the anointing and the discerning of spirits to get to the truth.

I have experienced prophets who say they are sold out for God: prophesying and prophecy coming to pass preaching and praying, and yet active in homosexual acts. How could this be, I would ask, and God would say to me in his word:

"For the gifts and calling of God are without repentance."

Romans 11:29

One does not need to repent for the gifts that God has given them to work in their lives.

Lifestyles are not deterrents to the calling on your life.

However, you will be judged according to the way you use the gifts and calling that God has given you.

The danger of active homosexuals in the church is the tendency for them to prey on new believers and believers who are in a weakened state, believers who want to live of the truth of God but have had experience with the homosexual lifestyle. They are tender in Christ and vulnerable to the attacks of the enemy. Left to the craftiness of elder believers who know the way but are engaged in this lifestyle, young believers are at risk of falling back into their homosexual ways.

Not only that, but these same gay males marry our women who are unaware of their previous and current lifestyle, because unless they are completely delivered, homosexual males, or anyone for that matter, are not able to give a testimony of deliverance. Therefore, they live a life of wolves in sheeps' clothing preying on our woman and bringing home diseases to their wives and children, because they don't want to tell the truth about their lifestyles. Yet they are able to come into the house of the Lord and praise him as if they did nothing wrong, and in them is fulfilled the scripture:

"As a dog returns to his vomit, so a fool returns to his folly."
Proverbs 26:11

These compromise the integrity of the church and make a mockery of the divine order set forth in the word of God, and though they come to church and participate in the service of the Lord, some of them still maintain some connection to that lifestyle. They maintain a friendship with a partner or friend in that lifestyle, and as soon as the opportunity arises, they run right back to it and put Jesus to open shame.

You can no longer look at a man and visually see whether or not he is gay, because these guys look like, act like, and in public live like heterosexual males. They love football, basketball, and baseball. They can hold a conversation about women, and if you have no discerning of spirit, you could be deceived. However, if a conversation develops about gay males, they will usually be quiet, or they will be unreasonably verbal about it.

For example: Suppose, ladies, that you are walking down the street with your man whom you don't know is having homosexual relations. Walking past you is a noticeably gay male, and you begin to giggle at him (the gay male). However, your man begins to say how much he hates "faggots," to the point where he expresses anger about it in a manner that is unlike what you had previously experienced with him. This man protests too much and is possibly having a homosexual experience.

A man with no homosexual experience is not concerned with a gay male. He is not threatened by a gay male and therefore would not get angry at seeing one. If your man has expressed this with you, you should investigate to see what the real deal is. You see, the only time a heterosexual gets exceedingly angry with a homosexual is when a homosexual approaches him in a sexual manner.

Gay males make their intentions known by the way they look at another male. It's called cruising. It is usually done when they want to meet someone or when they are just looking for sex.

Their eyes first meet, and there is a connection made. If one gets the message, they begin to move closer to one another. Lust begins to build, and each begins to touch himself, signifying what the intention is. This can go on for five, ten, even twenty minutes. Finally, after they get tired of checking each other out, or the lust reaches a point that they can't contain their desire anymore, one or both of them may approach each other, and they may go to one or the other's place; and lust is fulfilled. This somehow will lead to a relationship or a brief moment of sex.

This same action is going on in our place of worship, as quietly as it's kept. However, because we are so repressed about sex and are homophobic, we overlook it. These are tithe payers. Perhaps they are our best givers and they sing in our choirs, and because they come to church on a regular basis and marry our women, we call them delivered. They are at every prayer meeting, every Bible study, and perhaps never miss a choir rehearsal. God grant us people who have eyes that see.

These are in our churches because they think they can go about unseen. Some of them came into our churches serious about serving the Lord, but something happened along the way. They were tempted, persuaded, or deceived into thinking they could hide their sexual orientation, and in a small way, they have.

We must not dance over this issue. We must attack this spirit head on. We must break this spirit off our brothers and sisters and reclaim them back into the fold.

Let's send a message to the enemy: We will not allow you to steal the masculinity from our brothers anymore. We will not allow you to corrupt our young male children anymore.

> We will not sit quietly by and watch you change the truth
> of God into a lie.

Go ahead: Deny our right to the sanctity of marriage to one man and one woman. Yet we will still fight; we will still declare the name of our Lord! We will still preach that homosexuality is wrong, and that it is against all that is holy! We may not save all, but by all means we shall save some.

It is important that we not confuse the fact that homosexuality is a spirit, and it is that spirit we are against, not the man or woman who is trapped by this spirit.

Most people who are homosexual don't believe that they are held captive by this spirit, because they have lived with it most of their lives.

We must take our eyes off the person who has a homosexual spirit and place it on the spirit itself. Don't forget that our fight is spiritual, not natural.

Some of us who hated homosexuals before we were saved are still harboring the same feelings. This has no place in the church. We must learn to love the person but hate the spirit. We ought to get so angry at this spirit that we embrace our brother or sister. Defy the enemy who wants us to cast them aside; hate, mistreat, and demean them.

Remember that by love and kindness God has drawn us. We ought to draw them in the same way.

Chapter 4

I WANT TO BE FREE

"And ye shall know the truth, and the truth shall make you free."

St. John 8:32

It was helpful to me that I grew tired of the homosexual lifestyle and it catapulted me into the place where I could be made free.

Until you get tired of what you are into it is difficult to become free, because you still like what you are doing. It is still satisfying you. You are still getting something from it even if it is just a good feeling.

What you must understand is that God does not take anything from you; he receives of you. In other words, you must give to Him in order to receive of Him. So to pray, "Lord please take this thing from me," is not going to work, because you have to give it to him.

> God is not a rapist. He is not willing to take something you
> are not willing to give,

and in order for you to give anything to him, you must first be tired of it. So you must get tired of your lifestyle; you must get tired of sex your way.

> For unless you are tired of a thing there is no deliverance
> from it.

The woman with the issue of blood (see St. Matthew 9:20–22) got tired of being sick. She got tired of bleeding every day, of being weak and exhausted. She spent all her living on physicians and didn't get any better.

Finally, she heard that Jesus was passing by and decided to put her faith in Him and was made every whit whole.

The blind man at the side of the road (see Luke 18:35–43) heard that Jesus was passing by and refused to remain silent. He cried out to the Lord, and the Lord heard his cry and the blind man received his sight.

> You too can be free and completely whole by placing your faith in Jesus Christ.

To get you to the place where you will get tired, God often allows uncomfortable things to come into your life. In other words, your comfort zone becomes uncomfortable.

For example, when I started to get tired of homosexuality, there seemed to be more difficulties in my life. Loved ones that I thought were on my side were not on my side at all. All my familiar friends weren't around anymore. The more I sought them the more disappointed I got. The people who said they loved me turned around and left me, and my comfort zone was shaken. God knows how to get your attention. So by the time deliverance drew near no one had to ask me, "Do you want to be free?" because I didn't have any choice but to get free. There was nothing endearing me to my lifestyle anymore. There was nothing holding me to those friends anymore. There was no one to convince me to stay in that lifestyle.

You know how it is. You're on the brink of deliverance, and the person you are in a relationship with don't want you anymore, but as soon as you decide to go back to God then that devil wants you back. Now they want to start kissing on you. Now they can't go five minutes without you being in their presence. The devil is a lie. Pack your bags, baby; you're on the brink of deliverance. You're about to be made free, and the devil knows it. He's trying to stop your breakthrough. He's trying to keep you in bondage, and God wants to set you free. He's been waiting for you for a long time to get into the place where he can deliver you. Don't let the devil stop your blessing.

You've been tired a long time. You've been frustrated a long time. Tell the devil, "You're not stopping me this time. I'm pregnant with deliverance, and deliverance must come forth."

So I got tired. I threw away all numbers, letters, and pictures of people I knew were still attached to the homosexual lifestyle. I moved to another city, because I wanted to stay free. One of the first things God will do after you receive your deliverance is to separate you from influential distractions.

The Bible says:

> *"Death and life are in the power of the tongue: and*
> *they that love it shall eat the fruit thereof."*
>
> *Proverbs 18:21*

So I began to speak out my deliverance because Job 22:28 told me:

> *"You shall also decree a thing, and it shall be established*
> *unto you: and the light shall shine upon your ways."*

So I declared it, I decreed it, and I believed it.

Go ahead, start decreeing your deliverance, because it belongs to you; it is in God's will to deliver you. The enemy will try to persuade you that you can't be delivered; it's a lost cause. You will always be gay; you will always be addicted to sex; you will always be defeated. But this is a lie from the pit of hell. If He delivered me, He can deliver you. Is there anything too hard for our God?

It is now fourteen years since I've been free. In a span of three years my youngest son died at the age of eight, my brother in Christ whom I counted as my natural brother died at the age of thirty-eight, and lastly my mother died. My oldest son was briefly taken from me. I lived for almost a year without electricity or water. It seemed as if I couldn't find a job. My name was scandalized, my testimony was used against me, and those whom I thought were my friends lied about me behind my back because I trusted God and refused to give in. I told God I would never give up; I would never turn back. Come hell or high water I would live for Him and him alone.

So now some of you sit out there, or maybe you are reading this book, and you won't be made free, because the prospect of you living without frightens you. The prospect of living without someone frightens you; therefore you give in and you live beneath your God-given privileges, lying to yourself and saying things like, "I'm alright; I'll be OK," and knowing you are hurting and scared. Even some of you who are living with AIDS won't come to God to let him deliver you because you love what you are doing. Sex has you blind, and some of you have married just because you didn't want to have an urge and not have someone there to scratch it for you. The devil is a lie.

Marriage is not a cure for sex. Marriage is not a cure for homosexuality. Marriage is not a cure for lust. You need to be delivered, because as soon as you get the right itch, you will be right back out there (if you ever stopped) engaged in the same activity, making excuses because you couldn't tell the truth to yourself in the first place. This is why we have a church full of people who are hurting and in despair. Their marriage is gone, their home is broken, and a relationship they thought was strong is over, all because someone couldn't tell the truth in the first place.

Come on! Is there anybody tired of the devil? Is there anybody tired of being one of his pawns in a deadly game?

Hell is real, and unless you want to live there for eternity, you'd better fall on your face and cry out to God.

Deliverance is only in the name of Jesus.

> *"Neither is there salvation in any other: for there is none other name under heaven given among men, whereby we must be saved."*
>
> *Acts 4:12*

The devil has deceived you, making you think that good life is good pleasure. There is no life without Christ. Why would you live in torment when you could be free?

> When you can't control your own urge, that is torment.
> Therefore, you are a slave to your next urge.

The Bible says:

> *"Know you not, that to whom you yield yourselves servants to obey, his servants you are to whom you obey; whether of sin unto death, or of obedience unto righteousness?"*
>
> *Romans 6:16*

If you are bound by anything, you are servant to it. A person who is addicted to drugs is a slave to the drug he takes, and therefore he will steal to get it, lie, sell his body, sell his child, and even kill to get it.

I had the opportunity to feel what possession feels like. God allowed the enemy to attack me in my sleep, and for a moment, I couldn't do anything on my own. This spirit took over my motor functions, and I couldn't move my hands as I wanted to, or even say what I wanted to. I was completely enslaved in my own body, and this is what the enemy is doing to some of you. It may be on a lesser level, but the effect is the same.

All you have to understand is that God loves you and wants to make you free and make you whole. You don't have to be bound by sex, by drugs, by homosexuality, or by lust.

You can be free; right now, wherever you are you can be free.

If the son make you free, you shall be free indeed.

St. John 8:36

Be free in Jesus's name.

Watch what you allow your eyes to see. The media is putting a pristine face on homosexuality. You can't turn on the television without seeing two men kissing. You can't go to the movies without some reference to homosexuality. They are making homosexuality a household name, having gay males dressing up as heterosexual males all in the attempt to make homosexuality more acceptable. And some of us sit down and watch this mess, because, oh, they have style, not understanding that you are allowing the spirit of homosexuality to invade your temple. The more you watch the more acceptable it becomes to you.

Once the Lord delivers you, you must protect that deliverance, because the devil is seeking an opportunity to pull you back into the lifestyle you were delivered from. This is true especially if you were recently delivered.

What happens is that the devil gets you to watch these things, and before you know it, lust starts to build in you. You start thinking about it in your mind, and before long you're back into it, and you don't know how you got there, but you have invited it in.

Each time you sit down and watch these shows you are inviting that spirit in. Then you begin to compromise on what you will allow. You used to rebuke the memory of a past lover; now you're lingering on that memory. Now you're smiling in the memory, and before long, you're wondering how they are doing. Then the devil has them call you, because though you threw away their number, they still have yours. Then when you come to yourself you find that you are right back where you started. You see, the devil can paint a beautiful picture, but he can't maintain that beauty.

You must protect your spirit. Even the music you listen to should be scrutinized, because these things carry spirits, and spirits are transferable. Be careful whom you allow to come into your private space.

It cost me to gain my deliverance. It cost me to be anointed, and it is too expensive to allow anything to come in and make me lose what I've gained. You have to cherish your freedom and be willing to do almost anything to protect it.

Paul stated in the book of Romans:

> *"Wherefore come out from among them, and be ye separate, says the Lord, and touch not the unclean thing; and I will receive you."*
> Romans 6:17

You have to separate yourself from people and things that will influence you to go back into what God has delivered you from. Don't settle for less than the best. You can do it, believe me. It is only hard when you don't want to do it.

There is nothing too hard for God. He is able and willing to make you free. Be free in Jesus's name.

Chapter 5
The Seven Signs of Homosexuality

"These six things doth the Lord hate: yea, seven are an abomination unto him:
a proud look, a lying tongue, and hands that shed innocent blood, an heart
that deviseth wicked imaginations, feet that be swift in running to mischief, a
false witness that speaketh lies, and he that soweth discord among brethren."
Proverbs 6:16 –19

My heart goes out to women who are looking for true men of God to be their husbands. The first mistake women make is looking for a man. I know that in the world we live in today, women believe that it is their time to go out and find their mates, but this is against the order of God.

"A man who finds a wife finds a good thing, and obtains favour of the Lord."
Proverbs 18:22

It is still a man's job to find you. Your job is to prepare yourself for his coming. However, some of you will continue to seek your own mate and will fall into diverse lust, even some of you who have chosen your mates and have found out too late that your husband is having homosexual relationships. There are seven signs of the homosexual spirit:

1. *Offensive about gay males*
2. *Gazes or stares at men*
3. *Frequent calls from one man*
4. *Conversation changes*
5. *Slight changes in body movements*

6. *He wants to sodomize you (women)*

7. *Prolonged time in prison*

Some of these signs are very difficult to pinpoint, because they are subtle and you have to be looking for them to notice them. One of the last things a female thinks about when she starts to date a man is that he might be gay or that he sleeps with men, especially when the outside paints a picture of a heterosexual male. However, in these days this should be the first thing a woman thinks about before she gets involved with a man. This means that she will need to take more time during the courtship to get to know her perspective mate.

Now what you must understand is that you are dealing with a spirit, and spirit begets spirit. This is the same as saying, "Birds of a feather flock together." That is to say that a man who appears to be completely straight will hang together with other men who also appear to be straight, but they will have sex with completely gay males, even if it is just oral sex.

There is a mindset that says that it is possible for a man to have sex with a man and not be gay.

> In my book, if a man allows another man to touch him in a
> sexual manner he is a gay male.

Let's stop all this degree of homosexuality and call it what it is. We use degrees to make us feel better about what we are doing. So a straight male has sex on the down low with another man, and he is not gay; he is just a man who has sex with men. The devil is a lie. When two men come together sexually, they entertain the spirit of homosexuality, period.

> The spirit of homosexuality will not allow you to have
> partiality. What you will not give it takes.

All right, so there are seven signs to look for in determining if your man is having sex or has the potential of having sex with a man.

OFFENSIVE ABOUT GAY MALES

This is what I spoke about in an earlier chapter. When you and your potential mate, husband, or the man you are sleeping with out of wedlock are walking down the street and see a gay male, you begin to laugh or talk about him. But your man begins to get angry and starts to say how much he hates "faggots." Look a little deeper, because your man is having sex with a man.

If it seems like he is overly verbal about it. The gay male has gone about his business, and your man is still talking about it; your man is having sex or has had sex with a man. Don't just overlook it.

Homosexuality refuses to be silent or unseen.

What he is saying to you is that he doesn't like an outwardly gay male, but his anger about it gives him away. Your man may not have sex with an obviously gay man; however, he is having sex with a man.

In the homosexual lifestyle, there are various categories of homosexual males. Most gay males will fall into one of these categories.

These are:

Queens - Men who want to be, dress like, act like, and take on the role of women.

Butches - Men who like sleeping with men but will maintain their male qualities. They only sleep with queens and keep the role of a man.

Then there are men who I like to put in the category of:

Straight gay men - They like to sleep with men, but they want them to look like men. No dressing in women's clothing; no walking, talking, or gesturing as women. This is not the man living on the "down low." This man is gay, and he knows it. However, in order not to be classified as a gay male, men who have sex with both sexes and are not married have been termed "**Bisexuals.**"

GAZES OR STARES AT MEN

Most men won't admit it, but we look at men, not in a sexual manner. We might like what they have on, or maybe they look sharp and we admire that about them. True brothers sharpen true brothers. Thank God for real men of God.

However, when a man is prone to being attracted to men his gaze may be short. You can identify it; it is the way a man looks at a woman when we like what he sees. As with women, they are more prone to look at a man who looks appealing. He is handsome or well built. They like the way his butt is shaped, or even the way he walks. You know we all have our preferences.

Men are no different when they are attracted to men sexually. Just because they are attracted to men doesn't mean they are attracted to all men. They have preferences. The point is that men who are sexually motivated to look at men will do it more subtly, especially if they don't want you to know they are doing it. However, there are ways to detect them.

Whereas men who are attracted to women may gaze at them for long periods, men who are attracted to men have several short quick glances. For example:

Let's say that you are in the grocery store with your man friend, and you two pass a man who passes on your man friend's side. The two men's eyes meet each other, and an exchange is made. You never see it, but that quickly they have "read" each other. In a quick second they know if they are going to get together or not. You continue to walk, not knowing what has just transpired. However, your man friend is now on the prowl. He has you on his arm, but he is looking for any opportunity to see this man again.

You two are now at the register. You are talking to him, and you hear him answering you, but he is concentrating on the guy who is behind you the same guy he had a visual encounter with not ten minutes earlier. You are talking to him, and he is giving the guy behind you eye service. He is seducing this guy with his eyes, and you are none the wiser. You look up at him and see his eyes turn to meet yours. What was he looking at? Are you sure it was the magazines?

FREQUENT CALLS FROM ONE MAN

As a relationship grows between males that are in a sexual relationship, they will begin to call each other often. This may not seem strange to you because it is a man who is calling. Women usually tend to get suspicious when another woman calls their man's cell phone, beeper, or home phone. However, they rarely pay attention when a man is calling. Perhaps he has introduced you to a man who calls every day, maybe twice a day or three times a day. He told you that they were friends and explains to you how they met (usually a half truth). You don't question it, because the last thing on your mind is that your man is sleeping with another man. No, not your man; you were so very careful. You think you know the signs to look for. Gay people are feminine; they have limp wrists; they walk funny and talk funny and even look funny. They don't get married to women; they don't even like women. These are complete misconceptions.

When men call each other, and they are in a sexual relationship, they talk different. It is as if they are talking to women. Their voices change, as if they are in a romantic mood. However, they will not allow themselves to talk this way in front of you, so you have to go in another room and listen to his conversation. If you pick up another phone extension in the house, you will find that the other guy is talking more sensually than your man is leading you to believe. However, your man is responding in a way so as not to notify you of the true conversation.

So the guy on the other end says, "I love you, baby."

Your man or husband will respond, "Me too."

When you don't hear what the other guy is saying it seems as if they are talking about something completely different. Sometimes to make you less suspicious your man will even let you talk to the guy. It is all a plot to keep you in the dark.

CONVERSATION CHANGES

This is less recognizable, but when so-called straight men hang out with gay males, they believe that nothing has changed about them, but there are subtle changes in their conversation that have taken place that they may not be aware have happened. Only if you have been around gay males would you even notice it. Gay words tend to creep into their conversations. They may not know it is happening; but believe me, it happens.

SLIGHT CHANGES IN BODY MOVEMENTS

This one is difficult to see, because men who are trying to hide their true sexuality will work hard at hiding this. However, if you look very closely and study their movements, you may see very small evidence of this, especially if your man is receiving (being sodomized). There may be something in the way he moves his head that reminds you of a woman, or maybe the way he reaches for something. As already stated, this is very difficult to notice if he is trying to hide his sexuality. This excludes men who have been delivered, as they will possibly exhibit some feminine gestures.

Please understand that men who appear to be straight will not go out and date men who are obviously homosexual. They will date guys who are as obscure as they are. They want someone who will fit into their world. Now, in the dark they may have quick encounters with obviously gay males, but this will not lead into a relationship. You see, they will want to keep up the persona that they are straight men. Therefore they can marry and still have relations with their friends.

HE WANTS TO SODOMIZE YOU (WOMEN)

Once the spirit of homosexuality has entered a person and they open themselves to this spirit and begin to engage in sodomy with a man but have not been delivered from that spirit in their heart, there is a chance they will want to have sex in a woman's rectum. Also, if a man is attracted to men but has not yet engaged himself with a man, he may want to experience sodomy with a woman first.

Your man will usually have this conversation with you to see if you are open to this kind of sex. Let me just say that your answer should be emphatically no. You have no idea what you could be opening yourself up to. Spirits are transferable, and once you open yourself up to this kind of sex, you could be welcoming in several other spirits with it.

Sometimes men will ask you to do this in the attempt to have sex with you but resist the possibility of getting you pregnant. However, this does not stop you from contracting sexually transmitted diseases. In addition, if you let him do this to you, what's to stop him from doing it with a man if the opportunity arises?

PROLONGED TIME IN PRISON

More often than not, men who have been in prison for long periods have had sex with another man. Locked prison cells with no contact with woman and growing desires are nesting grounds for homosexual sex. This is not to say that it can't be avoided; however, the odds of this are very slim.

Let's understand that men are sexual beings, and when God is not in control, they crave sex on a regular basis. Having had the opportunity to get sex on a regular basis and being faced with not having sex for a long time can make men desperate, and desperate men do desperate things.

What I don't like is when men who have been in prison for years come out and act as if they had no sex with men. They don't tell the women they are sleeping with that they have had sex with men; in fact, they even lie about having sex with men. I don't understand why, because unfortunately, there are many women who have low self-esteem who would gladly sleep with these men if only to have a man in their life.

When a man and a woman have sex, they are not just having sex on a natural level but on a spiritual level also. Now the spirit of that man enters her body, and everyone he has had sex with enters her body.

In other words, when a man is sodomized by another man, the spirit of the man who is sodomizing him enters his body, and the two become one. When the man who has been sodomized goes and has sex with a woman and has an ejaculation, his spirit along with the man who has sodomized him enters that woman. Not only that, but the spirit of homosexuality has now entered her body also, because spirits are transferable. Now she has to deal with his mess, her mess, and the man's mess who sodomized the man whom she slept with. Moreover, she may have to deal with feelings of now being attracted to women. Sounds confusing, but it is real.

Before you engage in sex with a man you need to know the facts.

> Pray and ask God for wisdom before you engage yourself
> to a man

you don't really know. Stop walking in lust, the spirit of seduction, and sinful desires and ask God to deliver you. If you know of someone who has been into homosexuality, make sure that he or she is delivered, and don't date anyone who has recently been delivered.

If you are recently out of a relationship, don't go right back into one. Allow yourself to heal, to forgive, and to move on.

This is not a time to experiment. This is a time to get closer to the Lord, to allow him to show you love, to allow yourself to fall completely in love with him. This is the perfect time to get to know God. He has been trying to get you to this place for a long time. Stop putting a man or a woman before the Lord.

There is one way to avoid the possibility of having sex with a man who is having sex with another man altogether:

Wait on the Lord!

Chapter 6

EMPOWERING OUR CHILDREN

"...I have written unto you, young men, because ye are strong, and the word of God abideth in you, and ye have overcome the wicked one."

1 John 2:14

I was raised in the time when parents didn't talk to their children about matters of the sexual body. I didn't dare tell my mother what grown men were doing to me, because you weren't allowed to speak ill of an adult. Besides, I was sure that if I said something, these men would say they didn't do it, and I would be counted as a liar. I was a liar; however, I would have been telling the truth, and no one would have believed me. Therefore, I had no power to express myself.

I was frightened back then and didn't speak unless I was spoken to, because that's the way I was raised. I certainly didn't talk about the changes that were going on in my body, because that would have made me seem fresh. There was no man around to teach me what my body would go through or what I was experiencing at the age of thirteen. Therefore, I experienced sex on my own, in the dark, driven only by very active hormones that were now awakening in my body. Masturbating to get a release; playing with fire and not even knowing it.

Certainly, no one was around who believed in the spirit of the word to teach me what God had to say about the human body, or what this organ flapping between my legs was meant for. Nor did anyone teach me the pitfalls of engaging in sex without proper knowledge of what the consequences were.

What my mother said to me was not to date a particular girl, because she would get me into trouble. Now let's be real. That was not enough for me to stop seeing anybody. If anything, I would tell my mother that I wouldn't see her anymore and sneak and see her anyway, because I had begun to identify sex with love.

Sex is not love. Sex is not a prelude to love. Sex was designed for marriage between a man and a woman to help them be closer to each other. It is a gift from God for marriage only.

> However, as with all things holy the devil has taken sex and corrupted it into what it is today: mindless, selfish, unholy, meaningless, and corrupt.

The scripture says:

> *"My people are destroyed for lack of knowledge,"*
>
> *Hosea 4:6*

Yet we put our children in danger every day by not telling them everything about their bodies, about the changes that will take place in their bodies, about sex, or about how to cherish their gifts of love that God Himself has given them. We leave them in the dark with no defense, and when they turn up pregnant or infected with a sexually transmitted disease we want to be embarrassed. However, they can't be blamed for something of which they had no knowledge.

Before we are able to drive a car, we must first take a written test to get a permit. Then after a period of time we must take a driving test to make sure we can drive properly and safely before we are given a license to drive. Yet we give our children no test, no preparation before they go out and engage in sex. There are no classes on how to operate this machine that has a life of its own. There are no classes at home to teach them how to avoid predators that are out to take away what they are not willing to give.

We can't give them the spiritual side of sex and relationships but omit the natural side. Whether we tell them or not, nature itself will allow instinct to kick in, and by instinct they will know what to do in that moment. However, they will not have the proper knowledge to make informed decisions.

I started telling my sons about sex before they started school. I gave them the proper names for their body parts. As my oldest son came of age, I taught him what his body parts were for. I gave him God's insight about sex and marriage, starting from when he was young, because I didn't want him to make the mistakes I did. I taught him how important it was to wait until he got married to have sex, and every now and then I still ask my son, who is sixteen years old during the writing of the book, "Are you still a virgin?"

I empowered him to say no to anyone who may try to touch him inappropriately. I gave him the power to talk to me, leaving the lines of communication open. Sometimes he tells me too much, but I thank God because he is comfortable enough to come and talk to me.

I remind him about the dangers of having sex at an early age: pregnancy, sexually transmitted diseases, HIV, and AIDS. I told him who he was, I told him how much God loved him, and now that he is saved and filled with the Holy Ghost I still tell him to be careful. I can't be with him all the time, but I can intercede for him in prayer.

I even told him to be careful around men. I told him things like when he was in the bathroom (if I was not with him) to lock the door behind him. If you can't lock the door, go into one of the stalls and lock the door. If you do use a urinal, make sure no one can see your penis, and leave as soon as possible. You just can't leave anything up to chance today.

Now this does not mean that he will not have sex before marriage, but at least he can make an informed decision. No one will pressure him into having sex. If he decides to have sex it will be his decision on his terms, and he will be well prepared. However, I gave him options to protect himself in the event he does fall into temptation.

Love wouldn't allow me to leave him with no defense. Love wouldn't allow me to let him find out about sex and his body the way I found out about them.

> An occasional sermon from the pulpit is not enough to encourage our children to treasure their bodies as the temples they are.

We tell them that sex before marriage is sin, and it is. We have occasional speeches about HIV and AIDS and other sexually transmitted diseases, but we never speak about protection. We use fear to convince them of not having sex; however, teenage pregnancy is rising in the church at alarming rates. We have debates about whether we should tell our sons about condoms or not, and in the meantime our daughters are conceiving and bearing children, contracting sexually transmitted diseases, and having their dreams delayed or shattered.

In a perfect world, we could tell our children not to engage in sex until they are married, and some of them would listen and heed our words. However, what do we do about the rest of the group that doesn't listen, or doesn't have Christ in their lives? Do we just leave them to the wolves and not give them options to protect themselves? Even some adults don't heed the word and continue to engage in premarital sex. They have not allowed God to deliver them of the lusts that continue to oppress them.

Our children are encumbered with peer pressures, the desire to be loved, fear, helplessness, despair, homosexual feeling, and the desire to be accepted. Dealing with these fears, our children can become vulnerable to the tricks and traps of the enemy and therefore fall by reason of despair.

It is amazing to me that even in the twenty-first century we as parents still find it hard to speak about sex to our children. We can talk to them about the members of their bodies, but when it comes time to speak to them about having sex some of us seem to fall short.

Living in fear that they will have sex, we make a decision to not tell them the truth, thinking that if nothing is said about sex, they won't have sex. However, sex is in the eyes of our children from the moment they start watching television. Even cartoons are not safe anymore, and by the time they go to school even if you didn't tell them about sex their peers will.

Our children are living with sex every day, and silence won't make it go away.

Don't let the world name our children. Don't let the world tell our children who they are, or what they can or cannot be. Give them the voice they are looking for. Empower our children to be strong in the Lord and in the power of His might. Don't just tell them not to have sex. Give them options and expand on their dreams, and God will bless you with the answer.

Who are we waiting for to do it? If we don't warn them about unforeseen dangers, who will?

Demon spirits are real, and they are after our children. The Bible says:

*"The thief comes not, but for to steal, and to kill, and to destroy: I am come
that they might have life, and that they might have it more abundantly."*

St. John 10:10

The enemy is trying to steal the souls of our children. We can't allow this to happen.

There are children who have been molested, raped, or propositioned to have sex, and they are afraid to come and speak to you. Even some of your boys who have been molested by men are afraid to come to you, because they are afraid of how you will respond. They have never heard you speak on such things, so they don't know what to do. Now they have grown quiet. They are not the vibrant, fun-loving children you once knew. They begin to have problems in school. Their grades start to slip. When he or she used to sit with the family, he or she now spends more time alone. They are dying silently, and you don't know it.

You see how important it is to teach our children about the dangers of sex, to empower them before they leave the comfort of our homes and go out to school or in the neighborhood without knowledge?

> We can't afford to pick and choose what we tell our children
> anymore;

not in these times anyway.

However, it is hard to teach children something we have not learned. If you are still engaging in sex before marriage, why are you expecting your child not to? If you bring more than one man home in the course of a month, what are you teaching your daughter? Today more than ever, we must live the life we preach to our children. Children are not robots; they learn by example. What are you teaching your child by the things you allow?

Chapter 7

ON THE DOWN LOW

"Be not deceived; God is not mocked: for whatsoever
a man soweth, that shall he also reap."

Galatians 6:7

It is amazing to me how acceptable being on the down low has become. Even being a homosexual these days has become so acceptable that you can't turn on your television set and not see some reference to homosexuality. Talk shows have gotten on the bandwagon, making it even more acceptable, no one considering the pain that has been born by women and men left in the wake of their mate admitting they are on the down low.

Being on the down low is not new. It's been going on for years. It is only becoming known now with a more fashionable name. Anytime your husband or wife goes out and engages in sex with someone else, they are on the down low. You just don't know about it. Deception is what being on the down low is all about.

The only reason one even comes clean about being on the down low is because they have been caught. Writing a book about it after one gets caught does not make them some kind of hero. It doesn't comfort the person who has been wounded by their selfishness.

Any sex that is not in line with the word of God is about self. Self-gratification is the number one reason why most men and woman can't be faithful. It is one of the reasons why marriages have come crashing down, friendships have been dissolved, and relationships have come to a screeching halt.

Most of us in the church are into self. This is why we can't see more deliverance in the church. Some of us have not yet learned how to be sensitive to our brothers and sisters.

Now let's deal with men on the down low. For some reason, we seem to think that men who are married and are sleeping with men are the worst things in the world. However, I am reminded of a scripture that states:

> *"And Jesus answering said unto them, suppose ye that these Galileans*
> *were sinners above all the Galileans, because they suffered such things?*
> *I tell you, nay: but except ye repent, ye shall all likewise perish."*
> *St. Luke 2—3*

Jesus was referring to an act of violence toward a group of Galileans by Roman soldiers. He makes a reference that says that because these men suffered such things does not mean that they were gravely unrighteous, or sinners, but that we all need to come to repentance. The act of being on the down low is no worse than having sex out of wedlock. It all needs repentance.

In order to understand men who are on the down low you must understand the nature of the spirit. As stated before, lust is the driving force behind all sexual encounters outside of the will of God. This is signified by the scriptures:

> *"But every man is tempted, when he is drawn away of his own*
> *lust, and enticed. Then when lust hath conceived, it brings forth*
> *sin: and sin, when it is finished, brings forth death."*
> *James 1:14*

Let's understand that in order for a man to sleep with or have sex with another man there must first be an encounter with the homosexual spirit and lust. No man just decides to have sex with another man. This spirit works on a man and breaks down the line of compromise.

I am not talking about a man who has had to deal with this spirit most of his life. I am talking about a heterosexual male who for curiosity or perhaps because you have denied him sex more times than he could stand has chosen to allow a man to perform oral sex on him once.

Does this excuse him? No, by no means does this excuse him. However, if a man, or a woman for that matter, does not become free of lust before they are married, lust will permeate their lives throughout their marriage and leave the door open for advances from someone else. If a man has allowed another man to perform oral sex on him once, he will be open to it again.

For the most part, men on the down low have had previous encounters with men, usually before they got married. These men were bisexuals. They enjoy having sex with both sexes. However, when they get married, they neglect to mention this fact to their fiancé and become men on the down low.

> Being on the down low is only being on the down low when no one knows you're on the down low.

Once the cat is out of the bag, you are simply a man having sex with a man with no excuses for your action and nothing to hide behind, no cloak for your sin. As it is written:

> *"If I had not come and spoken unto them, they had not had sin: but now they have no cloak for their sin."*
>
> St. John 15:22

In other words, though we think our behavior is private, it is actually open and in plain view. If you are reading this book and engaging in this activity, you have now been exposed. You now know the truth and can't hide behind ignorance.

Please don't think that women in the church are immune from being trapped in this situation. Women are not immune to lust. This is why we have women in the church getting involved with the wrong men,

> so full of lust that even the pastor couldn't convince them
> that they were making a mistake.

Although we would love to blame men for the state of many women today, the truth is that women are playing a greater role in being caught in the situations they find themselves in taking it upon themselves to find a mate. What are you looking for? Be very careful; you just might find it. Ultimately we are responsible for our own actions; therefore, it is our actions for which we will be judged.

Do not make the mistake in thinking that being on the down low is an isolated case. There are possibly more men on the down low in the church than could ever be in the world.

I have met men who were married and were having relationships with men who were not called men on the down low at the time. These were men in the church. They held offices. They are musicians, prophets, and ministers with wives and had wives oblivious to their secret lives.

No, men on the down low is not new. It is like a plague spreading ever so quietly, and it is not noticed until someone dies. This is not the person you believe to be gay. This is not the person in the choir that you poke fun at because he acts like a woman. You see this man in service every Sunday;

you may be asking God for him. You introduced your girlfriends to this man. This may be your dream guy, because even in the church we doubt the virility of someone's testimony. Are you scared yet?

No one ever thinks this will happen to them, yet there are many woman, and possibly men, who can testify of this very thing.

Do not be high-minded, but fear.

> It is in the church where most of this is being played out,
> mainly because the church is where demons come first.

The devil is trying to persuade you to turn back and turn aside. He is not concerned with them in the world. They already belong to him.

He is looking for you: you who are so convinced that you're delivered but have not been tried in your faith yet; you who say, "I could never do that," and yet you have not conquered fornication; you who are married but can't stop lusting after someone else's prize. Have you never read the scripture that says:

> *"Wherefore let him that think he stand take heed lest he fall."*
> *1 Corinthians 10:12*

This spirit is like a bullet; it does not have a name on it. Everyone is a target, and the only way to escape it is through the blood of Jesus.

Beloved, being on the down low is not strictly a homosexual case. If someone's wife is having a sexual relationship with another man, and it is unbeknownst to her husband, that wife is on the down low. She is creeping out on her husband, and her husband is in the dark.

Being on the down low could refer to heterosexual and homosexual alike. However, because it has been referenced to married men sleeping with men, we breathe as if with a sigh of relief, thinking we are safe when we are not safe.

Who knows what trouble will breeze by your home leaving adultery behind. Whether your mate sleeps with a man or a woman and you are left in the dark, your mate is on the down low. It means that he or she is keeping it on the DL.

Please understand I am not trying to minimize the issue. I'm showing you how broad it really is. The enemy wants us to concentrate on one segment of the population while he ravishes the areas less watched.

Again, this is a stronghold, and you can't just wish it away. This demon needs to be cast out.

Chapter 8
ARE YOU SURE HE'S GAY?

"Judge not according to the appearance, but judge righteous judgment."

St. John 7:24

Not every man who has feminine gestures is gay. What has taken place in this man's life is that he was raised by a woman or women who had for one reason or another no man around. Therefore this man took on their feminine gestures.

So that you understand, some women who have been mistreated by one or a few men tend to be angry will all men, and if they don't get delivered they can exhibit this hatred to her sons.

Then when they conceive a man-child by a man who has mistreated them, they don't want anything to do with that man and don't want the man-child to have anything to do with that man or any man for fear the son will learn the same behavior. What the woman has done now is cut off from that child any way of him finding out about himself.

Other women have had their men die on them, leaving them with a man-child to raise and with no other men around willing to take time with that child; the child is again cut off from finding out about himself.

In the course of time, this man-child grows up and exudes natural male activity and functions. He runs constantly; he wrestles with other children, perhaps even girls; he tumbles a lot, destroys his toys, maybe a few pieces of furniture; and he touches himself. While these behaviors may need to be curbed, the woman, not understanding, punishes that child for a behavior that is natural to him. Over time, he learns not to do the very things that are in his nature to do. With no male figure around for him to emulate, he takes on the nature of his mother, aunts, sisters, or any other female around.

As he attends school, he is labeled a faggot, gay, girl, and homosexual. Men who come around sparingly start to tell him to stop switching and walk like a man. His family asks him why he walks like a girl. Soon his self-esteem diminishes, his self-respect dwindles, his self-worth is gone, and he begins to exhibit self-hatred. Because he has been misunderstood for so long, he becomes sensitized to the advances from other men. Yet he finds the strength in himself to resist temptation.

However, sometimes the abuse is so strong that by the time this young man is propositioned his spirit has been broken. In order to receive some kind of acceptance or love he is willing to deny his own sexuality. We all just want to be loved.

This person was not gay. He had no desire to sleep with another man. His affections were in the right place. When he was asked, "Are you gay?" his answer was no, possibly with tears. However, because of his mannerisms he is identified as a homosexual, and no one believes him.

> If enough people put you down long enough, you can begin
> to believe the lies they say.

All of this could have been avoided if that mother who hated men allowed a man to take her child and spend time with him. Likewise, the woman whose husband died had a responsibility to put a man in this child's life. Male children need men around.

As I stated in my testimony, there were no men around on a regular basis to teach me what it means to be a man. In addition, my mother didn't allow me in those early years to do what other boys in the neighborhood were doing, and when I exhibited normal boy behavior, I was punished for it. Therefore, because there was no male around, I took on the emotional baggage of my mother and exuded female mannerisms.

Forget the fact that I was touched by men at an early age. If there were men around I could have learned how men behaved and excluded that behavior.

From the moment a male child is born, he needs the attention of his father or another male who will take time with him.

Mothers, if there are no men around, you must find a man willing to spend time with your man-child on a regular basis. Stop using these kids as pawns. You think you are helping this child, but you are destroying his very nature. Find a big brother program with men who will mentor your son. Find a man, dig up a man, but get a man into this child's life.

Now you must be careful of the man you allow to be in your child's life. Make sure you know him well, or if it is a big brother program, make sure you get references on the brother who will spend time with your child. There are predators out there waiting to get a hold on your son. So while you are willing to allow a man to spend time with your son don't be so trusting that you allow any man to take your child.

It is common knowledge that children are mostly molested by people they know. Be very careful. Pray about it. Ask your local church if there are men willing to mentor your child, and check them out before handing your child over to them. If this is not possible, ask men you know how you can promote healthy male experiences in your son's life.

Women cannot be fathers; nor can men be mothers. God has given each one of us a role to play. It's when we change the roles or the order of God that we get into trouble. Then our children are left holding the emotional baggage from all the mess we arbitrarily placed on them.

Unfortunately, one must truly get to know the brother who has feminine gestures but is not gay to find out where he stands. It is not visible to the eye, as he will have the outward motions of a woman. His voice may be deep, but it will have a women's ring to it. However, usually he will not have any gay friends. He may stay in the company of women, because men can't or won't understand him.

He is not threatened by gay males, so he won't be offensive about it. In his heart and mind he is a man misunderstood by fear or ignorance. He has the desires of a man, and he expresses them. He will be very attracted to women and verbal about it.

He glances at women, not men, and if he does look at a man it is because he likes what he is wearing, not what he has between his legs. If he has regained his self-esteem and self-worth he will approach women with confidence, and women will respond to this.

He will be well dressed, well groomed, and perfectly put together, having learned from his mother. However, this is true of the gay male also in most cases.

The bottom line is that we must be careful when we are classifying every male who exhibits feminine gestures as homosexual. Sometimes this is not the case. These gentlemen cannot be held responsible for something they had no control over. They can't help how they were raised or who was responsible for raising them. Even some homosexuals were brought into this lifestyle through no fault of their own, but the good news is that God is able to deliver, make free, and make whole.

Chapter 9
Sold Out or Fed-Up

"But as many as received him, to them gave he power to become
the sons of God, even to them that believe on his name."

John 1:12

Many people are addicted to the homosexual lifestyle. They are comfortable and feel complete in the lifestyle they have chosen. Therefore, it can be difficult to speak to them about Christ and the deliverance of homosexuality, because they love it so much. In other words, they have sold out to the homosexual lifestyle, and no manner of discussion could make them give it up. Only Jesus can change their heart and mind.

Any thought that one could be delivered from homosexuality is emphatically denied, and for one to stand up and say, "I have been delivered from homosexuality," is met with criticism from the gay and lesbian community. The person who is delivered is thought to have been brainwashed or still engaged in homosexuality instead of having a real encounter with the Lord.

The fact that these persons go on to have productive lives living as heterosexuals is not considered. Rather, homosexuals are looking and expecting them to be caught in a homosexual act so as to have some proof of their farce. Thus, a lie is believed rather than the truth.

For one to say, "I have been delivered," is to say that there is something wrong with homosexuality and there is a cure. We have already discussed that most homosexuals feel that they were born that way and that it is a part of their makeup. It is in their genes; gay blood pumps through their veins, and their heart beats to the music of YMCA. Nothing could be further from the truth.

As stated before, homosexuality is a spirit. It is conceived by the devil to destroy the image of God in the case of men and to destroy the image of man in the case of women. This is why men should despise two women coming together sexually instead of rejoicing in their lust.

Two women coming together is confusion to God, but it should be abomination to men, because woman was given to the man. She is made in the image of him (the man). Please understand that women are helpmeets, not slaves. She is to be at her husband's side, not his backside.

The bottom line is that people who have sold out to the homosexual lifestyle will reject my testimony, because it is a witness against what they claim to be true. However, there is only one truth.

Jesus is a deliverer of homosexuals.

Therefore, if Jesus delivers homosexuals, homosexuality must not be of God. For Jesus said:

> *"…Every kingdom divided against itself is brought to desolation;*
> *and every city or house divided against itself shall not stand."*
> *Matthew 12:25*

That is to say: If God created homosexuality, why would he then deliver someone from it? He would be working against His own kingdom. If he delivered someone from something he created, he would be working against himself. In other words, he would be divided against himself, and his kingdom would not stand.

However, we know that God does not work against himself. he is too wise for that, so he must be working against Satan, and homosexuality must be of the devil.

There are people who are living under the influence of homosexuality who are being devastated by the daily life of homosexuality. They are in pain daily dealing with something they have no control over, because this spirit is a stronghold. These people have been raped, molested, gang raped, and abused. Some of these will dedicate their life to the homosexual cause. Others will participate in homosexuality, but almost as an unwilling participant. They may feel that something is wrong, but the drive to commit these acts is stronger than they are.

These people are looking for a way out. Some of them are even in your congregations, and they are crying out for help, but they are warring with a spirit that refuses to let them go.

This spirit wars in the spirit of your mind and affects the body through lust. It feeds off carnal desires that are inside each of us, and these people are fed up. Some of them have committed suicide to escape this spirit and the rejection of their family and friends. Others, like myself, have attempted suicide but were unsuccessful, because God had a plan for their life.

My message to these people is that Jesus is able to set you free. I'm a living witness. The pain and despair you feel is nothing compared to the joy that awaits you in Jesus.

Jesus Christ, a man approved of God, came and dwelt on the Earth. He performed many miracles, healed many diseases, and set many captives free. For the purpose of saving and dying for the world he came, and He opened a door for us to receive of His power.

This power is available to each one of us today. He is still healing, he is still saving, and he is still setting the captive free. I invite you to meet Jesus right where you are and in the condition you find yourself in. Receive of his love and be healed in the name of Jesus Christ.

You may not know it, but while you were reading this book, even reading this chapter, God has begun to deliver you. The weight and stench of rape and molestation has been removed from you. You don't have to live with the memory of it anymore. You don't have to live with the pain and disgrace of it anymore. The Lord has made you free. Your desires are beginning to change, your mind is being renewed, and your hope is being restored. I decree it, and it is so. Praise him and bless his holy name.

So What About Marriage?

Therefore, if any man be in Christ, he is a new creature: old things are passed away; behold, all things are become new.

2 Corinthians, 5:17

Obviously, I believe that anyone who has been bound by homosexuality can be made free. My testimony is a testament to that fact. Therefore, if a woman meets a man who has been in the homosexual lifestyle, and they want to get married, they should. However, it is very important that the man be very honest with his potential mate. It is likewise important that he be honest with himself.

> One of the greatest things in this world is to see a man regain his masculinity.

Some people are delivered instantly, while others are delivered over a period of time. Whether instantly or over a period of time, all who have been delivered from homosexuality need to spend time alone to be perfected in their deliverance. The reason for this is that the enemy is not through with you yet. There must be a time for the trial of your faith.

Please understand: If Christ has made you free you are free indeed (see St. John 8:36). However, it is still possible at the early stages of deliverance to be persuaded to return whence you came. Therefore, for a few years after your deliverance you should not think about getting married. In these few years, you will be engrossed in the heat of battle.

You see, the enemy will use the person you absolutely can't say no to. You know, that last person who moved you the right way and is constantly in your thoughts. Before you get married, these things must not move you anymore. You have to get to the place where even the memory of a past relationship doesn't move you anymore.

It is important that the delivered man not rush into marriage. Loneliness is a poor reason to bring someone into your struggle to maintain your freedom. Until you have conquered your insecurities and fear of turning back you should not get married. No one should have to put up with your indecisiveness.

As stated in an earlier chapter, the fear of being alone is what makes us rush into marriage. Therefore, when we are delivered the first thing the Lord does is separate us from almost everyone. In this separation is when loneliness sets in and our warfare begins.

For some delivered homosexuals it takes time to even be attracted to women. Having been attracted to men for years, and perhaps never having been with a woman, it will take time to master this ability. For fear of being rejected by saved men, delivered men may be curious about hanging with men and will still gravitate to women as a comfort zone. However, the best way to learn about being a man is by hanging around men.

On the flip side are the delivered bisexual and the man on the down low. They are comfortable with woman and therefore will have no problems being attracted to one. However, caution is advised: Do not engage with any woman in the church until you know for yourself that you are delivered.

We overcome by the blood of the lamb and the words of our testimony (see Revelations 12:11). The best way to find out if a man is truly delivered is if he tells the testimony.

> When someone will risk exposing himself or herself to humiliation, that's when you know they are delivered.

Ladies, do not marry any man who will not expose himself to you. If he holds back on one thing, he is holding back much more.

If anyone is delivered from bondage, the first thing they will do is confess it openly for joy of being made free. Consider the man laid at the gate of the temple at Jerusalem (see Acts 3–11). Peter and John on their way into the temple stop and take time to heal a lame man who was asking for alms. Peter and John healed the lame man in the name of Jesus. After being assisted to his feet, the man begins to worship God for his deliverance.

This man didn't stop to think about praising God for his freedom. He leaped up right where he was and started to worship and praise God for his ability to walk. No doubt he told everyone along his journey what the Lord had done for him. It is the same with someone who is delivered from homosexuality.

It is completely up to the individuals if they want to get married. However, I believe that it would be prudent of a newly delivered male to wait on marriage. Allow the Lord to bring you through the tough times you will go through before bringing someone into the chaos. You are delivered, it's true; however, it can be a process getting to the point where you are not moved by homosexuality at all.

I can't say how long a delivered male should wait to get married. For me the ideal time is when you can look at a male you would have been attracted to and feel nothing; when you can think about two men kissing and it disgusts you; when the very thought of two men being together sexually makes you sick. The time frame is different for each individual.

Just remember that marriage is a sacred and holy union. It is not meant to be entered into on a whim or to escape the unpleasantness of loneliness. Each individual should be complete in themselves before entering marriage.

He Is Calling You

"Repent and be baptized everyone of you in the name of Jesus Christ for the remission of sins, and ye shall receive the gift of the Holy Ghost."

Acts 2:38

It gives me great pleasure to tell you of the good news. The winds of change are blowing your way. What could not be spoken has now been revealed. The shadowed places have now received light.

If you are reading this book, then you have been touched by this spirit in some way in your lifetime. Maybe you know someone who has gone through some of what you have read. Perhaps you have gone through or are going through it yourself.

Maybe you have read this book and feel the Lord tugging at your heart. You have read this book and you were touched by words of deliverance. Perhaps you are tired of your lifestyle and want to be free. It doesn't have to be homosexuality or lesbianism, but perhaps you have a problem no one knows about. Perhaps you have raped or been raped. Maybe you have molested someone and want to be made free.

Maybe you are living on the down low, and no one knows about it. Know this: There is nothing hid that shall not be revealed (see Mark 4:22).

Jesus does not want to expose you. He wants you to expose yourself:

"Confess your faults one to another, and pray one for another, that you may be healed. The effectual fervent prayer of a righteous man avails much."

Jesus is present to heal you of past hurts, past pains, misunderstandings, and self-hatred. Your past can be wiped away, and you can start with a clean slate.

You have tried everything else, even getting married. You thought that if you just get married your life would change. Maybe you won't need sex as much. However, what you have found is that it didn't get better. It only got worst. Now you're not just dealing with your own bondage; you also find yourself engaged in a completely new kind of hell. There is no escape other than Jesus.

Perhaps you are saved, Holy Ghost filled, baptized in the name of Jesus, but you are still bound by things from your past. Perhaps you are a backslider and want to return home, but you don't know if you can. Let me tell you that Jesus loves you and you can always return to him. He is married to the backslider, and He is waiting on your call. His ears are open, and His arms are stretched out wide. Come to Him and believe.

If you desire Jesus as your personal savior pray this repentance prayer:

"Lord Jesus, I'm a sinner. Forgive me of my sin. Come into my heart; free me from within. In Jesus's Name, Amen."

Congratulations. If you have prayed this prayer you are now saved. You are now a part of an elite group of people, a peculiar people a royal priesthood (see 1 Peter 2:9).

Now find a congregation in your area that preaches the true word of God, where you can be taught and nurtured in the truth. Then be baptized in the name of Jesus (see Acts 2:38). Begin to read the Bible for yourself, and the Lord bless you richly.

Glossary

Bisexual – a single man or woman who has sex with both sexes.

Butch - a homosexual male who has sex with a male who classifies himself as a queen. Butch men do not receive.

Calling - purpose; a reason for being; a divine mandate (preacher, teacher, prophet, or helper, etc.).

Cruising - when two men are checking each other out or are attracted to each other.

Deliverance - to be made free from.

Enemy - the devil. Anything against the truth of the gospel.

Faggot - a homosexual, usually a reference to men. A man who sleeps with men. Viewed as disrespectful to the gay male.

Heterosexual - a person who only has relationships with people of the opposite sex.

Homosexual - a person who only has relationships with people of the same sex.

Laying - a biblical term for having sex.

Lust - to crave something. Strong desire.

On the Down Low - married men or women who sleep with both sexes.

Queens - men who feel like and want to be women. They only receive.

Receive - men who are being sodomized.

Repent - to ask forgiveness.

Straight Gay Men - men who sleep with men but act like heterosexual men. This is a gay male. He will most likely not sleep with women.

About the Author

James Bligen was born December 29, 1964 in the Bronx, NY. The only child of his mother, James started life like most boys do; happy and care free. However, He would endure continued molestations from the age of four, until the age of fifteen catapulting his life into chaos, and confusion. Filled with rage, anger, self hatred, and self doubt James spent years trying to overcome his past.

Today James is born again, blood washed, and spirit lead. James' mission is to promote and expand the kingdom of God. He is mandated by God, to build the church of God with flesh and spirit. James has the move of God in his soul, earnestly desiring to see believers living to their potential. Moving beyond the realm of the natural, and deep into the realm of the spirit. James' heart is for those who do not know the Love of Jesus in the pardon of their sin.

Look for more from this dynamic man of God in the future.

www.ingramcontent.com/pod-product-compliance
Lightning Source LLC
Chambersburg PA
CBHW021233280526
45784CB00005B/2089